ROBERT
PAUL
SMITH'S

LOST
&

FOUND

ROBERT PAUL SMITH'S LOST & FOUND

Illustrated by
Gerald Gersten

CHARTERHOUSE
NEW YORK

ROBERT PAUL SMITH'S LOST & FOUND

An

Illustrated Compendium of Things

No Longer in General Use–

the Hatpin,

the Icebox, the Carpet beater

and Oven

Household Possessions

They Don't Make That Way

Any More

ROBERT PAUL SMITH'S LOST & FOUND
Copyright © 1973 by Robert Paul Smith

Library of Congress Catalog Card Number: 73-79960
Manufactured in the United States of America
ISBN: 0-88327-020-X
Designed by The Etheredges

For Knox, without whom.

CONTENTS

13

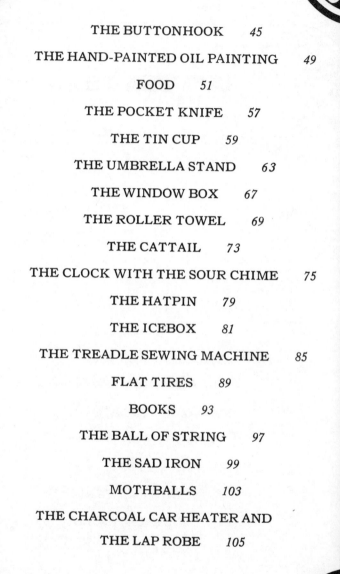

CONTENTS

13

15

ROBERT
PAUL
SMITH'S
LOST
&
FOUND

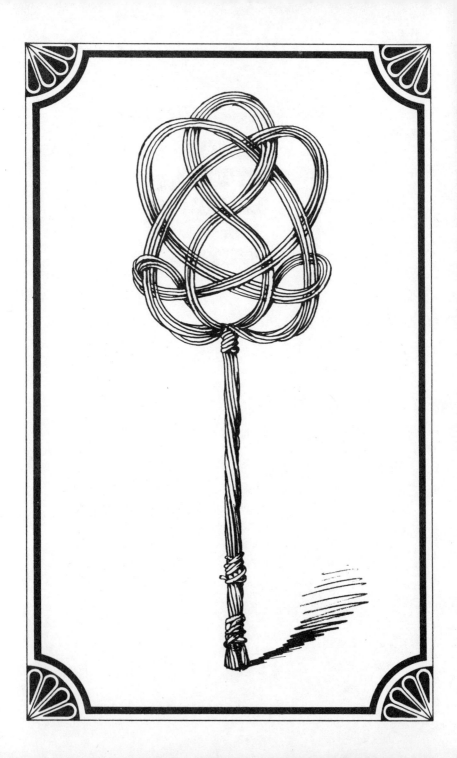

THE CARPET BEATER

This is a carpet beater. You took the carpet off the floor (Nobody had ever heard of wall-to-wall carpeting. Who in his right mind would *nail* a carpet to the floor—a carpet was a thing that sat fringe-to-fringe on the floor) and you wrestled it outside and boosted it onto the clothesline. (The clothesline was a rope strung from one post to another, and if the sun shone, whatever you hung on the clothesline would dry, and if it rained, anything you had hung on the clothesline would get wet. Other perils to anything clean hung on the washline were open

19

ashcans, high winds, vigorous dogs who ran with a great deal of knee action, small friendly children and larger malicious children. The closest thing we had to a tribal dance in those days was the rites of the sudden downpour as every lady on the block rushed to get her wash in.)

Well, if there was no wash on the line, and there was an active male in the house, and if it was the proper season, you took the carpet out and hung it on the washline and you took the carpet beater (you found it, always, hanging from a nail at the top of the cellar stairs) and you hit that carpet with that carpet beater.

According to age and familial status, every stroke of the beater was (a) a home run with three men on base, (b) a blow for liberation from algebra, (c) an intemperate reply to the head bookkeeper, (d) certain loud communications to a wife.

Independent of emotional attitude was a large cloud of dust, which did what dust always does: floated around for a while, and then fell down in a thinner layer on a larger space.

Since you shared your particular dust with the general neighborhood, inevitably some of your dust settled on someone else's carpet. Then somebody else hauled a carpet out and hung it on a clothesline and beat it with *his* carpet beater, and got even with *his* employer, or *his* wife, or *his* geography teacher.

Aside from all the release from tension thus provided, there was one more virtue to a carpet beater. You didn't have to clean it.

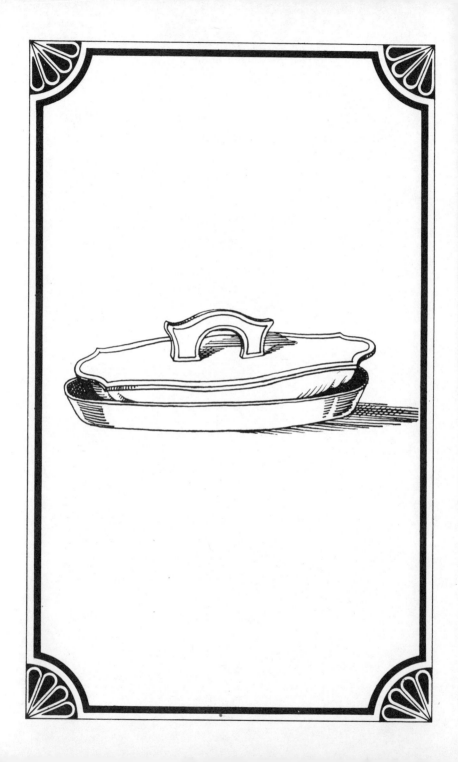

THE
NAIL BUFFER

This is a nail buffer. It was made of celluloid (celluloid was a plastic that was invented before plastics were invented), or ivory, or tortoise shell, or silver, and I suppose, in some places, solid gold.

Whatever it happened to be made of, the working part of it was made of something called shammy, which we were later informed was really spelled "chamois." (It is curious, but true, that another thing having to do with nails was also spelled in an incomprehensible way. That was the pummy stone which sat on the side of the bathroom sink and abraded off fingers whatever kind of dirt could not otherwise be removed. There are people who think it was a "pumice" stone, but they're the kind of people who never used a pummy stone.)

Assuming your hands were clean and you were a lady, your next move was to the nail buffer. Ladies took it by the handle part, and shined up their nails by stroking them with the shammy part the same way that gents shined their shoes. I think, but am far from sure, that there was some kind of powder that ladies sometimes dipped the shammy (or chamois) pillow in, perhaps some very fine kind of powdered pummy (or pumice).

In any event, and you must simply take this on faith, ladies' shining nails were nail color, and had moons. (Moons were those things at the bases of the nails which ladies used to push back their cuticles with a kind of little hoe to show more of, instead of covering up the whole nail, moon and all, with those different color paints they have now.)

There was also a kind of white pencil that ladies used to shove under the working ends of their fingernails to make sure they were white and clean.

This pencil did not work unless your nails were clean to begin with by determined work with an orangewood stick (which was neither orange-colored nor wood, but a stick made of the wood of a tree on which oranges had once grown, and match that for exotic).

If you were a small boy and had dirty fingernails, the dirt was between the white pencil and your fingernail, and the white pencil did no good at all. The way small boys knew this was that they tried. Most of them also tried buffing their nails with a nail buffer, but they never told anybody about it.

Until now.

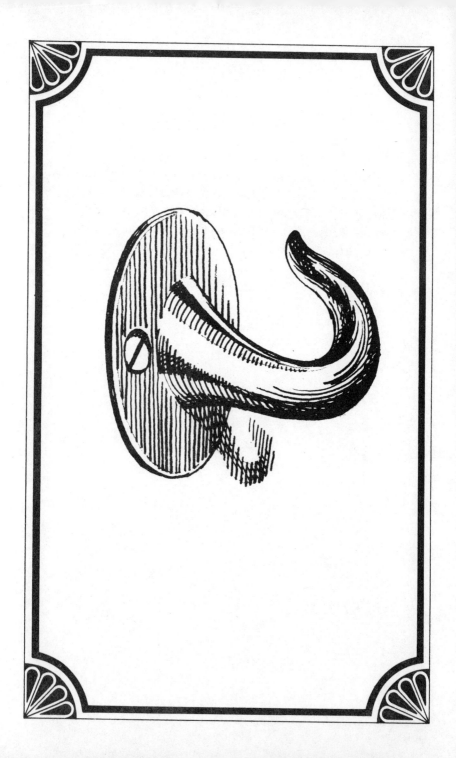

THE RAZOR
STROP HOOK

This is a razor-strop hook. It is that thing sticking out of the bathroom wall, if you have an old house, that you don't know what it is, but you keep hitting your elbow on. The reason you don't know what it is is because you don't know what a razor strop is. And that's because you don't know what a razor is.

You likely know what a safety razor is, unless you're so young you think an electric razor is a razor. It is not. Nor is a safety razor a real razor.

A real razor is a straight razor. It is also known as a cut-throat razor.

Any man who shaved with a straight razor was a man with unlimited confidence in himself and in the future. He also believed in the staying power of a good piece of steel and in his ability to keep a cutting edge on same.

He did this by stropping his razor before each shave, first on the canvas side of the strop and then on the leather side, and then, in some extreme cases, on the palm of his hand. The strop was on a swivel hook which fit on the razor-strop hook that you hit your elbow on.

Any man who had the guts to sharpen and face his own personal guillotine each morning of the year started each day as a hero. What happened when the safety razor came into fashion was that heroes went out. Emerson never could have written "Self-Reliance" after being abraded by an electric razor.

THE COALBIN

This is a coalbin. The coalbin was in the cellar, where you went when life was totally unbearable. You sat on the coal in the coalbin, and it shifted some under your bottom with a mournful sound. Properly, you sat with your head in your hands and your elbows on your knees, and got black all over—as black as your mood. It was the best place in the world for figuring how sorry they'd be when you had lived in the coalbin for fifty or sixty years.

The coalbin had other uses. It was a place to throw things that you shouldn't have had in the

first place, didn't work in the second place, and would be hollered at in the third place for having had in the first place.

The coalbin was also a way of getting into the house when you didn't want anyone to know you were getting into the house. It also provided the fuel for the furnace that, more or less, heated the house. Coal didn't put itself into the furnace the way oil, or gas, or electricity does now. There was an intermediate step between the coalbin and the coal furnace which was you and a shovel, or Pop and a shovel, or John Gherardi and a shovel. (All furnace men were named John Gherardi, and they always arrived early in the morning on a bicycle with a racing saddle and no coaster brake.) You should also know about the ash sifter, a sheet metal mechanical wonder that you set on top of an ashcan. You shoveled ashes into it from the bottom of the coal furnace and turned a handle. This agitated the ashes so that they were partially all over you and once in a great while a piece of unburned coal was sifted out and held in the sifter. At the end of sifting, say, three cans of ashes, you might wind up with three cents worth of coal, which went back into the furnace.

There is more to be told about coal furnaces. In every coal furnace there was something called a damper. A damper was something that never worked quite right. The way people now talk about the proper proportions for a perfect martini, they talked then about a furnace damper. There was a mysterious ceremony performed every night by one accredited necromancer in the house, which involved putting ashes on top of the glowing coals. I don't know why this was done, because by the time I was old enough for my initiation into the mysteries of the furnace—just at the age when I was ready for the ritual ash and fire dance—we moved to an apartment. And to this day I have never quite grown up.

Lots of kids thought that coal grew in the coalbin, or that every house was built on a coal mine—until the day they heard a noise that was the most splendid and terrifying noise in the world. The noise cannot be described, except to say that it sounded like coal going down the coal chute into the coalbin. It is a simile that the world is poorer without.

There are some words that are going to be hard to replace, like ashcan, and ash man, and people who never shook down the ashes can never know how exactly a trumpet player missing the last note of a run is like a clinker in the grate.

THE RAG BAG

This is a rag bag. A rag bag is a bag that used to hang on the cellar side of a cellar door. It had a wire loop sewed in the mouth to keep it open, and bagged rags. There are only two things that can be done with a rag bag. (1) Put rags in it so that later on you can (2) take rags out.

A rag is any article made of cloth that isn't able to do what it did once. This having happened, it becomes an article made of cloth that can do anything. Once it was only a shirt; now it is a window-washer or a floor-cleaner or a sink-sanitizer. Once

it was simply a sheet; now it becomes a bandage or a kite-tail or a handkerchief.

People no longer have rag bags because there are factories now that go right ahead and manufacture rags without bothering to make them into shirts and things first, and they put them up for sale already sealed into pliofilm bags that, unlike rag bags, are very hard to open. It isn't surprising that a nation that devotes so much energy to by-passing the oldest established free rag-maker (man) has trouble with its gross national product.

It's also one more simile shot to hell. Unless you have seen an old-fashioned rag bag in full bloom, you have no adequate way of describing the way certain ladies look, or the way the inside of your head feels on certain mornings.

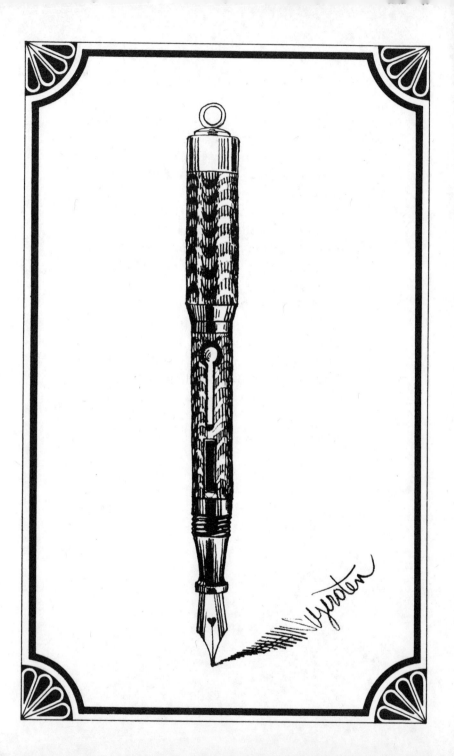

THE
FOUNTAIN PEN

This is a fountain pen. These days, you look in a desk drawer and there's a double handful of ball-point pens that work (to my taste, not very well) forever. If a ball-point pen doesn't work, you can dip it in lighter fluid or hold it in a match flame and it will start working again. I suppose there are people who throw pens away, but I don't know any. You probably lose them first, anyway.

When I was a boy—and the brontosauri were very friendly—Papa had a fountain pen, Mama had a fountain pen, and possibly big sister had a fountain pen. Unlike fountain pens, ball-point pens are common property—they'll go with anyone who picks them up. When I say that Papa had a fountain pen, I mean to say that that fountain pen belonged to Papa, and woe to anyone who thought otherwise. After using a fountain pen for a time, the tip wore down to exactly your personal angle, and not only did someone else using it find it refractory, Papa on regaining it found it a little askew. Borrowing Papa's fountain pen was a thing you did not do twice.

Mama's fountain pen was easier game. It was usually a desk model that swiveled on a green onyx base, but it was usually out of ink, so easy game or not it was useless. Sisters wore their pens on little blue ribbons around their necks, and they were as much jewelry as writing instruments. They had a tendency to be filled with green ink, and automatically wrote little circles over i's instead of dots.

Even if you had a fountain pen, you couldn't take it to school. Dip pens and pen-holders and ink were issued free, and it was the policy of the school that, since not every kid could afford a fountain pen, no kid could have one. In many respects, some principles of democracy were much more in evidence then.

THE
TELEPHONE DOLL

This is a telephone doll. It resembled, more than anything else, a perverted lamp shade. It came in two colors—pink and blue. (I do not mean pink or blue, I mean pinkandblue.)

The telephone doll was used to hide the telephone. A telephone came in one color, black, and it was considered, with some justice, ugly. (People considered, with some justice, all pieces of machinery ugly, and so either ornamented the machine with scrolls, birds, lions' feet, birds' claws, caryatids, eagles, sunbursts, cherubs, Moors' heads, naked

ladies, strong gentlemen in loin clothes, clenched fists, arms with bulging biceps, American flags, or hid it. You hid the telephone.)

The phone did not ring as often then, and you had enough time to pick up the telephone doll, set it down on the table, pick up the earpiece and hold it to your ear, pick up the mouthpiece part and hold it to your mouth, and speak to someone in a louder voice than usual.

Now phones come in pink and blue, and Lord knows what other colors, with little lights on them and push buttons that make entertaining noises, and one can converse in a normal tone of voice.

Except it rings more now, and we have to scream more often to persuade the person at the opposite end that we do not wish to buy any of that.

THE ATTIC

This is an attic. It is the place where writers write, painters paint, adolescent children go to give their *Weltschmerz* a fighting chance, furniture is put that is too good to burn and too dilapidated to sit on, ditto pictures of people who look familiar to you but whose names you do not know. In brief, it is the place where all people who cannot make up their minds, and all things that you cannot make up your mind about, live. If Dante had known about attics, he wouldn't have had to write all those cantos about limbo.

Ancient people, like me, do not know what the phrase "unfinished attic" means. It is like talking about wet water, or hot fire.

An attic is a sort of cellar, but it is at the top of a house, so that people become an uneasy filling between two slices of untidy impermanence. Contemporary houses do not appear to have cellars or attics. This is a snare and a delusion; they are all attic and cellar, except that the junk is new junk, and when it starts to block up the entrances, you move.

THE BUTTONHOOK

This is a buttonhook. A buttonhook is something that used to be used to button buttons on shoes. Buttons on shoes were things that were used to close shoes before laces were used. Laces were something that used to be used to close shoes after people gave up wearing boots, which were shoes that did not have to be closed because there was no way of opening them in the first place. (Sometimes they had elastic sides so they opened up a little bit.)

The reason you do not know what a buttonhook

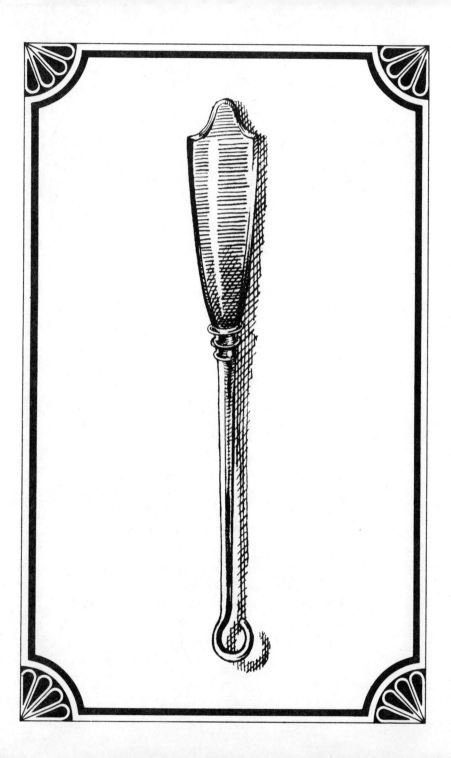

is is that the shoes you now wear either have (a) zippers or (b) elastic or are (c) loafers, which are very low boots that you don't have to close because they don't open up in the first place. The other reason you don't know what a buttonhook is is that you don't need one (if you are a man) to hook a dress collar over a collar button because you don't have that kind of collar any more, or because (if you are a woman) you no longer wear that particularly delicious kind of elbow-length kid glove.

On balance, these are the gains and losses: there are no more jokes about looking for a collar button under the bureau; ladies in evening dress are not as exciting as they used to be; men do not turn as red in the face as they used to; and you don't have a bootjack.

A bootjack is a thing that you used to use to take boots off with when you used to wear boots. If you didn't have a bootjack, your wife had to help you off with your boots. If you didn't have a wife, you had to holler for somebody else to help you off with your boots.

If nobody answered you died with your boots on and you became a legendary hero.

THE
HAND-PAINTED
OIL PAINTING

A genuine hand-painted oil painting was a picture of a lady or a man, or some cardinals in red robes drinking red wine out of ice-cream-cone-shaped glasses, or a big animal with big horns or big teeth, or a lot of naked ladies sitting around a Greco-Roman locker room, or an adorable little girl tormenting a kitten, or a St. Bernard dog, or some pigeons, or a little boy in his mother's bathrobe making believe he knows how to spin a top or ride a horse or be noble, or a couple of little boys with torn breeches eating grapes in the gutter, or more horses than you can count raising a lot of dust, or a bowl of wax fruit with or without some dead birds, fishes, and rabbits, or a building falling apart, or a man standing up in a boat, or falling off a horse, or dying on one elbow with a lot of rearing horses and smoke around, or dressed in a sheet making a speech with gestures to a lot of other people in sheets, or a man and a lady in shiny clothes getting ready to kiss each other, or a mountain seen from a valley or a valley seen from a mountain, or a whole mess of waves.

Maybe they weren't very good pictures, but at least you knew what they weren't very good pictures of.

FOOD

This is a bowl of wax fruit. A not uncommon artifact was the wax fruit that stood in a bowl on the dining room table. It was the most perfect-looking fruit that ever was. It was all a little over size and the vivid colors and perfect contours made it a model of what fruit ought to look like. The taste and consistency, however, left something to be desired. That is to say, it strongly resembled the real fruit of today.

Fruit was ever a chancy thing, it being local produce grown in a local orchard catch-as-

catch-can, not in the outdoor factories that send us our fruits and vegetables from clear across the continent and sometimes across the world. It was a gamble: sometimes it was green, sometimes it was overripe and usually it assayed fairly high in worms and other strangers. But when you got a good one, it was tree-ripened and full of sun, and the juice ran down your chin. And it was not improved the way so much fruit is today. A sickle pear (I know now it's Seckel) was supposed to be small and hard, bumpy and flinty. I was given one the other day that was beautifully pear-shaped, a lovely green with a red blush and there was that faintest hint of the flavor that made a Seckel pear a sickle pear. Sickle pears were in season for only the briefest time, coincident with Concord grapes, and they may not have been good for the bowels, but they were very good for the soul.

There used to be white peaches and yellow peaches. White peaches had the most delicate flavor in God's green world, and yellow peaches were very fuzzy, left your lip sore, and were mainly used by one's mother for canning. There are no more white peaches, except occasionally in cans from Korea. True.

There were two kinds of corn for eating on (off?) the cob, Country Gentleman and Golden Bantam. The Country Gentleman corn was white, the rows were uneven and straggled all over the cob. It was

53

more delicious than can be told. Golden Bantam was yellow, very even, and orderly, and it was what you ate when you couldn't get Country Gentleman. There is no more Country Gentleman.

There were bananas, and red bananas, and little tiny finger bananas. Now it's all bananas. With trademarks, yet.

All cooked vegetables were cooked until they could not be cooked any more. You knew there would be cauliflower for dinner half a block from home.

Turkey was once a year, and we were thrilled by it the first dinner, and loathed it by the end of the week, as it kept popping up in transparent disguises, just as it does now, but longer because the turkey was bigger. (I read recently that commercial turkey raising is only about thirty years old, so I suppose it would been more exiting if we'd known it was wild turkey, but nobody ever said so because apparently there was no other kind.)

Back then, food had to do with the seasons. You ate root vegetables all through the winter because that was all you could get. There were small individual seasons, too, when you ate the same thing every day because it was in season, not only vegetables, but smelt and shad when they were running. You ate rhubarb in the spring because it cleaned the blood (whatever that might be) and butter was almost white all winter long, and only came yellow when the cows went back to pasture greens.

So far as food went, then everything was good but not perfect, and now it is perfect but no good.

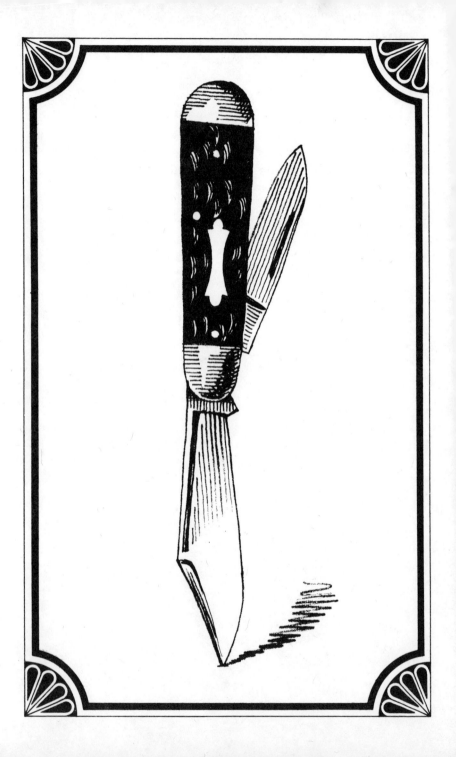

THE
POCKET KNIFE

This is a pocket knife. It was used to: sharpen pencils, cut chaws off a plug of tobacco, trim fingernails, peel apples and green branches, cut string, whittle peach-pit monkeys, open packages and blisters, make belts bigger or smaller, prune trees, sliver cheese, inscribe initials and messages on tables, desks, trees, fungi, fences, railings and wooden handles of hammers, rakes, hoes, ice-choppers, on pencil boxes, turtles, rowboats and handles of other pocket knives.

It trimmed, smoothed, roughened, notched,

planed, scraped, made holes bigger and pegs smaller, pierced, split, pried (with care), hammered (with the handle, with care). It was sharpened with spit on a flat stone, or with oil on an oil stone, and honed on the sole of a shoe when shoe-soles were still leather.

A man would no more leave the house in the morning without slapping his jacket pocket to make sure he had a knife than a commuter would leave home today without his tranquilizers.

If, tomorrow, you forgot your medicinal happy dust, and remembered your pocket knife, you could make yourself very tranquil by really sharpening a pencil, if you had an unmechanical pencil.

THE TIN CUP

This is a tin cup. It hung from a pump, or a faucet.
It was to drink from. It was public.

About the time the germ theory of disease
squeaked through into general repute, it was discovered that the public tin cup was a dirty thing.

Anybody who knew anything knew that this was
untrue; all people of any daintiness who used a
public cup habitually used the far side of the cup
to drink from, thus having the totally private use
of totally public cup.

It never occurred to any of us that this made

the private side of the cup the public side. If it had we would have all switched to the near side of the cup, thus having, once again, private use of a public utility.

Things were simpler then. People, too. (Water was much colder then, by the way.)

THE UMBRELLA STAND

This is an umbrella stand. It stood in the hall and was made of tin painted black with gold stencil designs, or it was made of wood in Mission style of fumed or golden oak, or it was a not very success-fully disguised piece of sewer pipe with a bottom on it. Dogs were always fascinated by the bases of umbrella stands.

Raincoats then were no more waterproof than they are now (no matter what the ads say) and in any event there was implicit immorality in allow-ing any article of clothing to get wet if you could help it, so you wore rubbers and a raincoat and a rain hat, and carried an umbrella over all.

A well-equipped umbrella stand contained a minimum of three umbrellas with wooden crook-handles, all enormous, old, valuable and black. (There was also a cane—or canes—in the umbrella stand.) In the kind of house where they played bridge, there was sometimes in addition a smaller umbrella, purplish and not quite umbrella-shaped, with a handle covered in leather, often not even crook-shaped, or with a small tassel. It was well known that in such houses, three times out of five, there was a lady who smoked cigarettes.

Umbrellas were unfurled only on the porch, and when wet were allowed to dry, open, on the porch. Once dry, they were rolled and placed in the umbrella stand. The only person in the house who could roll an umbrella properly was the father.

An improperly dried and negligently rolled umbrella became mildewed, was thereafter somewhat greenish-black in color, and whoever had done it wrong was bawled out. (Any male child discovered by his peers carrying an opened umbrella not in the company of an adult led, from that moment on, a life of degradation and misery.)

The man who came around to grind knives was also the man who repaired umbrellas, which seemed to me then (and seems to me now) a combination unlikely in the extreme, like a peanut butter and salami sandwich.

It is perfectly true, even though it was a staple of the funny papers, that at least once a year a kid jumped off a roof using an umbrella for a parachute, and broke something: an arm or a leg or an umbrella.

 # THE WINDOW BOX

This is a window box. When people *liked* their houses to bulge out here and there, lots of houses had bay windows. Below the bay window, there was an enormous built-in box with a lid, and on top of the lid there was an aggravation of cretonne, and on top of the cretonne there was a maladjusted child finding solace in the Doré illustrations of Dante's *Inferno* and the good daylight from the bay window. It was known for certain in those days that even worse than reading by artificial light was reading by a mixture of artificial light and daylight.

A child on the window box was assured of not being hollered at for ruining his eyes, particularly if he were smart enough to point himself on the window box so that the light came from over his left shoulder. (The worst thing of all for the eyes in those days was to read by a mixture of artificial light and daylight over the right shoulder lying down with rubbers on. All right, all I know is that you didn't see so many people wearing eyeglasses then.)

Sooner or later, whoever was sitting on the window box was chivvied off it to go out and get some fresh air. Under the lid lived ice skates, ball-bats, a butterfly net, a soccer ball, a fielder's glove, golf balls, balaclavas, a ball of kite string, large rubber bands, dog leashes, high sneakers, hockey sticks, and a large roll of friction tape.

By the time you got back to the window box and put back the stuff, closed the lid, smoothed the cretonne, and got out the Doré again, the daylight had gone and your ankles hurt.

THE
ROLLER TOWEL

This is a roller towel. It is a long loop or endless belt of huck toweling that hangs from, and rolls on, a wide wooden cylinder which in turn is held and pivoted between two brackets on a wall.

Do not confuse a roller towel with the machine one now finds in a public place, in which an incredibly long towel is endlessly and eternally reborn from a clean white magic metal box, so that the area you pull down is clean and untouched by any human hand prior to yours. It is clean, is there, is untouched by previous human hands provided

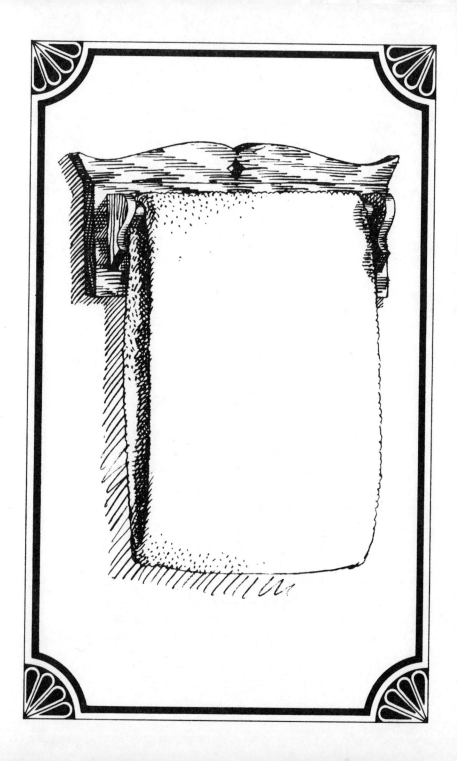

the machine is not out of order, the service man has shown up, and the magic box has not been replaced by an even more magical machine which purports to dry your hands by playing over them a jet of hot air. (This machine is a total surrender to the electronic cult, in which anything plugged in is by definition superior to anything not pluggable-in; it not only does not dry your hands, it also chaps them. There is no case on record of such a machine actually drying a person's hands without recourse to a handkerchief, shirttail, slip, or the seat of a pair of pants.)

A roller towel faced the fact squarely that a towel is something that is going to get dirty. It was arranged so that the finicky got a cleanish part, the slobs freewheeled, and the public-spirited changed the entire towel.

Some washroom philosophers saw in the roller towel a constant reminder of the undying myths: of the phoenix, of the snake that eats its own tail, of *yang* and *yin*, good and evil, night and day, winter and spring, Pluto and Persephone. The large majority of people saw it as a roller towel.

It did have one overriding virtue; it was always there. And it did not holler at you, "Blot, do not rub," or "Rub, do not blot," whichever it is, which does make rebels and felons of us all.

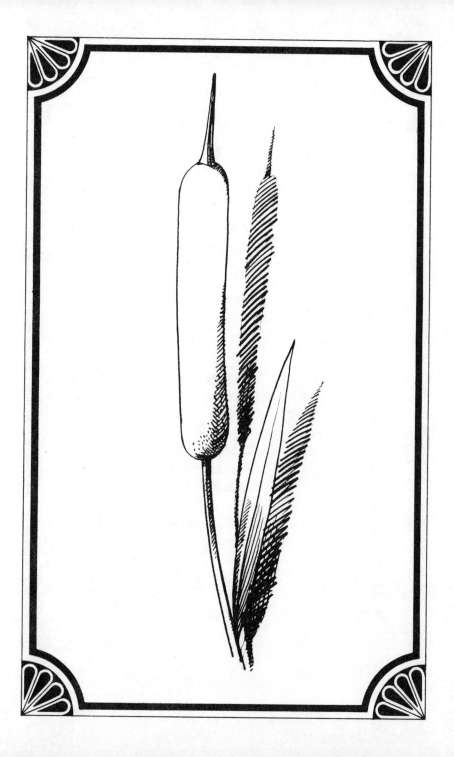

THE CATTAIL

This is a cattail. It grew in the swampy ground on the rim of that bog which is now a real estate development called Grassy Copse that you don't have enough money to buy a split-level house in.

Cattails were pleasant things to look upon and had three other functions.

Ladies of great artistic sensitivity let them dry, painted them with radiator paint, poked them into tall vases along with various other debris and became the cultural leaders of the community, including the Browning Society.

Small boys of less rarefied sensibilities and patience threw them at each other as spears.

Small boys with more patience allowed them to dry, soaked the heads in kerosene (you could tell the kerosene can because the spout was plugged with a potato), lit them, and found them splendid torches.

After a while, if not painted, thrown, or burned, a cattail became very dry and if you rubbed your hand over the bushy part, you could create a cloud of highly allergenic material, only we didn't know what allergenic meant then.

THE CLOCK WITH
THE SOUR CHIME

One of the signs of opulence in a suburban household was a large and expensive clock. Some were
grandfather clocks which stood in the hall and were
not expected to work, some were French clocks
of convoluted brass that stood under bell jars with
pendulums loaded with mercury or revolving
instead of swinging.

But by far the most common was a large wooden-
cased clock that stood on the mantle and had, more
or less, the Westminster chimes.

These clocks struck the quarters pretty well, if

a little off-key, but in almost every one, there was a really sour note that tolled the hours.

At a quarter to, you were put on notice that a gigantic clinker was coming soon, and you braced yourself for it. But by the time the hour came you had forgotten and your entire being was struck numb by a clam of enormous proportions. You sat and hoped that one day the clock would hear what it was doing and adjust the note, but it never did. It kept on insisting it was okay, for as many as twelve times.

It was never fixed, never replaced, and after a while you got so you'd have missed that sour chime. It proved something in the depths of your soul, although you never knew exactly what.

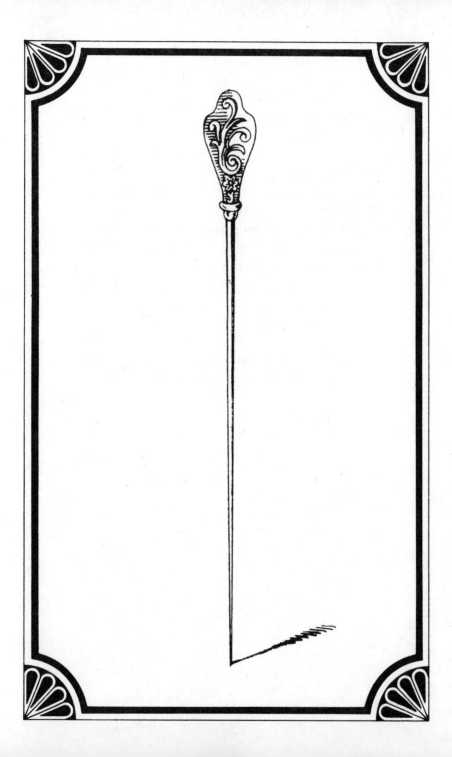

THE HATPIN

This is a hatpin. We first saw hatpins when our mothers were dressing to go out. First the hat, a complicated architectural masterpiece of stiffened cloth or straw was set on top of the head and patted into place. Then she took a small stiletto, often from between her teeth, placed the point on the hat, and drove six inches of cold steel straight into her skull.

Often she drove still another spike into her head. She didn't even whimper, and we assumed it was one of those mysterious things women could do, like filing fingernails and plunging their hands into practically boiling water.

Later on in life, when we read Shakespeare, we needed no notes on the bodkin Hamlet would use to his quietus make. He would borrow one of Gertrude's hat pins.

THE ICEBOX

This is an icebox, which is what members of my generation still call a refrigerator.

The ice came in big blocks, delivered by an ice-man with a horse and wagon. The ice was in very big blocks on the wagon bed, and there was a lot of sawdust around. This was still clinging from the ice house, where ice was insulated with sawdust, or it was put on the blocks in the wagon so they wouldn't stick together. You ordered the number of pounds you wanted, more in the summer and less in the winter, but I do not recall that it was weighed. I do remember that with an ice pick, the proper size block was outlined and magically separated itself from the bigger slab. The iceman wore a leather apron slung from his neck and over his back and he had a pair of ice tongs—a sort of big hinged pincers. These were dug into the block, it was swung around to his back and he carried it to the icebox.

, There were two doors and two compartments to the icebox, the upper for ice, the lower for food. The iceman horsed the ice into the upper part.

Iceboxes were not as cold as refrigerators are, which was good and bad. Things had more taste then, but they didn't keep as well. There were long, lively discussions at the table about whether the butter had really turned, or if you thought the milk had soured.

Ice water was generally considered unhealthy, which was just as well because it meant doing a messy job with the ice pick. (I remember trailing after a grownup to see the seventh wonder of the world, an oil burner, and the eighth, an ice cube.)

There are two more things to be said about the icebox. (1) Eugene O'Neill's *The Iceman Cometh* is going to require footnotes in a very few years. (2) As the ice melted, the water ran down into a flat square metal pan underneath it. At any hour of the night, somebody in some house was hollering

1, I forgot to empty the icebox pan!" You

leapt out of bed, went down the stairs as many steps at a time as you could. The icebox was usually in the back entry, and you knew immediately that you were too late as your toes crystallized and fell off, sounding a tiny bell-like scale.

It was a long way from the back entry to the kitchen sink, and as you lurched your way little waves of ice-cold water traveled across the shallow pan, up over the edge, and into your belly button.

You wet-mopped the floor, crept up to bed and swore never to forget again.

Three days later you forgot again.

THE TREADLE
SEWING MACHINE

This is a treadle sewing machine.

Its top was made of golden oak, its legs of cast-iron elaborated and filigreed. The treadle was also iron open work. There was a golden oak flap at either end which could be lifted and locked in place. There was a black enameled metal plate with gilt scrolls let into the oak top, to which the sewing machine was bolted, and the plate was hinged, so that the machine could be lowered into the top. With the machine down and the flaps up, it made a large table for laying out sewing work.

A mother could come in, put one foot on the treadle and the machine ran with a wonderful noise, (To this day, a good automobile mechanic will say of a properly tuned engine that it runs like a sewing machine.)

A small boy could sneak in, stretch his legs so both feet touched the treadle, and no matter what, the machine would run backwards.

Fifty years later, he realized that what he'd interpreted as an affectionate pat his mother gave the shiny silvercolored wheel at the right of the machine was really a push of the fly-wheel in the right direction.

FLAT TIRES

This is a flat tire. These days a lot of people have never changed an automobile tire. The tires are tougher, they don't keep their cars that long, and the roads are better. But way back when, a motorist was known not by the speed at which he could corner, but the speed with which he could change a tire.

You didn't change wheels then, just the tire. The first step was to jack up the car and that was the labor of Sisyphus with those old heavy motorcars. You had previously horsed off the spare, which was mounted on the rear of the car, or in a front fender-well. You took the wheel with the flat off, lay it flat on the ground and walked around on it to break the joint of bead and wheel. Then you took a tire iron and worked around the wheel to loosen the rim. Then you walked around on it. Then you used the tire iron. Then you swore. Then you mopped your brow.

You did this a great many times. Then the rim, a large flat split ring, jumped out and hit you on the ankle. Then you took the tire off. Then you horsed out the red rubber tube.

Then you did everything over again in reverse order, after patching the tube. This was done with a little C clamp flattened and enlarged on one jaw, on which you put a patch. You set fire to the back of the patch and it vulcanized itself permanently—well, sort of permanently—to the tube. Sometimes you patched the inside of the tire too. If it was a blowout, which shredded the tire, you put the patched tube inside the spare.

No matter which you did, the next thing was to pump up the spare. You did this with a hand pump. No one I ever knew had a tire gauge. You just pumped until the pump pumped up harder than you pumped down. It took a very long time.

This whole process was known as going on a picnic.

I have a feeling that the foregoing may not be

totally accurate. After all, I was small, the sun was hot, and I didn't do it—I just watched. I know I have left two things out; getting the rim back on, which I can't remember how it was done. And that when you once got the tire back on the wheel, you had to take it off again, because you hadn't remembered to have the valve sticking out of the hole in the wheel.

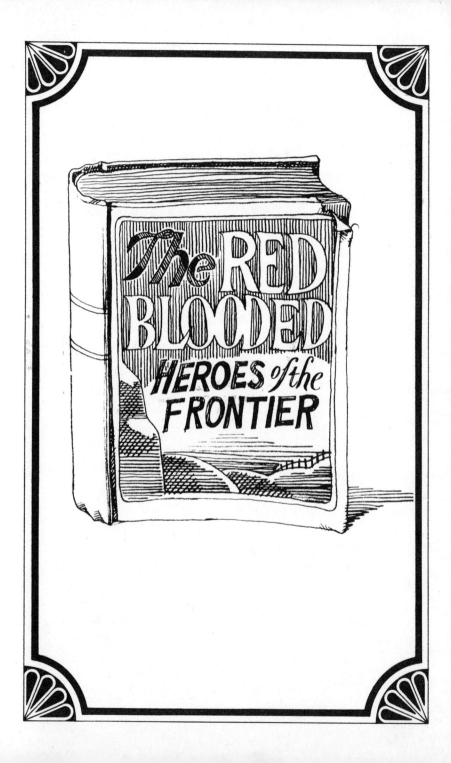

 **BOOKS**

This is a book. Books came in three flavors: Good
Books, Bad Books, and Library Books. It had
nothing to do with the moral tone of the books.
Good Books were the books you were told to read,
at school. Bad Books were the books suggested
to you by other kids. Bad Books were never
purchased, but were loaned and swapped from one
kid to another. They were really our only currency.
The market fluctuated in swapping, but Tom Swift
had a pretty steady market value, equal to three
Boy Allies or two *Motor Boys*. As far as we knew,

none of these books had ever been brand new, they were created second hand, with the spine shaky and various unidentifiable stains on every third page.

Library books were sometimes Good, sometimes Bad. On the Bad side was one entire shelf of Henty, and a lot of Kipling, and books like *The Boy Mechanic*, which told you how to build everything from a telegraph set to a hang glider. But most of the library books were Good.

Come to think of it, there was another kind of book, found in the home: Sets. A fond uncle once gave me the collected works of Mark Twain. I read from volume one to volume twenty-four and then back again to volume one for the next ten years.

I must have read such Good Books as *Ivanhoe, The Vicar of Wakefield,* and *The Mill on the Floss,* but I never did read any Fenimore Cooper. I announced in English class that he was dull, and that Mark Twain thought so, too. I was thrown out of English class but I never did read *The Pathfinder*.

In my small milieu we devoured *Tom Swift, The Boy Allies,* the *Motor Boys,* the Mark Tidd books, *Stalky and Co.,* but somehow none of us cared much for Frank Merriwell.

But the greatest of them all was Mark Twain,

and whatever education I received came from him. Just to show you how far you can trust an uncle, the following year my birthday gift was the collected works of Washington Irving.

THE
BALL OF STRING

This is a ball of string. The only place you saw a tailor-made ball of string was in a store. It hung over the counter in a black iron case made to look like a beehive.

The real triple-distilled ball of string was found in a kitchen drawer, along with candle-ends, rubber bands, smoothed-out sheets of used wrapping paper, three-in-one oil, pliers, a few screwdrivers and a corkscrew.

There must have been some time in the history of the family when there was not a ball of string, but by the time children came along, it was well established. Every bit of string that came into the house was carefully unknotted (cutting a string on a package would bring down an immediate lightning bolt on your head) tied onto the loose end of the ball, and wound in.

At first, this made sense—whenever you wanted a piece of string, there it was. But as the years wore on, it became an addiction. You would have a ball of string as big as your head, and the chance of using it up in anybody's lifetime was remote, but you kept on, long after the ball grew too big for the drawer and sat on the counter. I tell you true when I tell that sometimes the ball was passed on from generation to generation, and occasionally there would be a newspaper photograph of a dim old man leaning under the weight of a ball of string that had been in his family since Gettysburg.

I am still horrified by people who buy balls of string. I fear they will die in penury.

THE SAD IRON

This is a sad iron. The reason it is called a sad iron is not because it made women sad (although it did) but because at one time in the English language sad and heavy meant the same thing. It doesn't have a handle because that's the whole point.

You had two sad irons and when you thought one was hot (you started by setting them both on the stove, or stovelid, if it was that kind of stove) you hooked a handle made of heavy wire and wood into the slots on the top. You then held it up to

your cheek, to see how hot it was. (I was as stupid about this as I was about hatpins, I thought my mother was pressing it right onto her cheek, that it was another of the pain-defying things women were able to do.)

After a while the iron you were using got cold and you set it back on the stovelid, unhooked the handle, hooked it into the other sad iron and went on with the weary business.

MOTHBALLS

This is a mothball. It was a small white sphere of camphor, a little smaller than an immie. When the summer approached, all the really heavy woolen winter clothes, as opposed to the really heavy summer clothes like striped or white flannel trousers, were hung up in the closets and mothballs were stuffed in all the pockets.

The closet doors were closed and a concentration of camphor fumes was released strong enough to kill moths or a healthy Newfoundland. (I wonder whatever happened to Newfoundlands, by the way.

They were so common as to be almost synonymous with dog.)

When summer was over, the clothes were released, reeking of camphor and in some cases moth-hole free. The camphor balls had decayed somewhat, and stuck to the linings of the pockets and the ladies, no doubt intoxicated by the fumes, almost always missed a pocket or two, so that the whole country had a background noise of suddenly released mothballs falling and rolling down the aisles of movie houses, houses of worship, school rooms, and other quiet places.

The camphor smell was almost gone by the following summer.

THE CHARCOAL
CAR HEATER AND
THE LAP ROBE

This is a charcoal heater and a lap robe. Automobiles in those days had little grey cloth roller shades on the windows and little cut glass flower vases on brackets (although I don't recall ever seeing cut flowers in them), but they didn't have heaters.

You dressed for driving, in the warmest clothes you had. On the back of the front seat, facing you in the rear, was a long metal rod, and draped over it was a kind of rug, big enough to spread over everyone in the back seat.

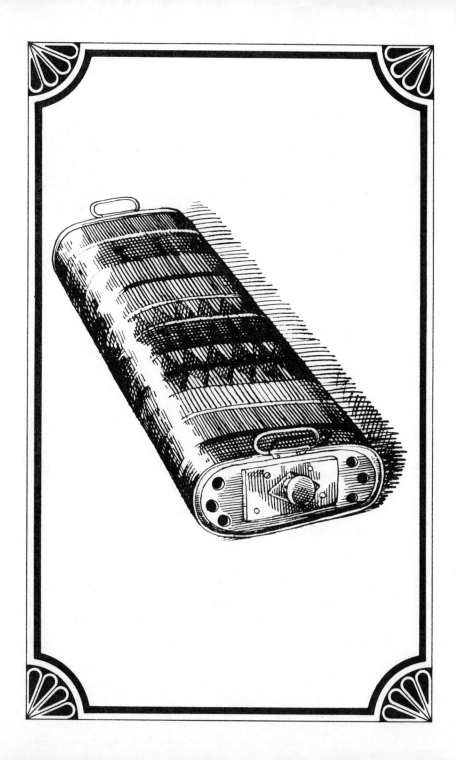

Usually this robe sufficed, but in extreme cold you got out the charcoal foot-heater. This was a hollow metal tube about three feet long, triangular in cross-section. The ends were pierced with a number of small holes and it was covered with carpeting. You put charcoal in it and then lit it, or maybe you lit charcoal and put it in the heater.

In any event, you put your feet on it. Your feet got terribly hot. You were, I realize now, also risking imminent death by asphyxiation, but at least you would go out warm.

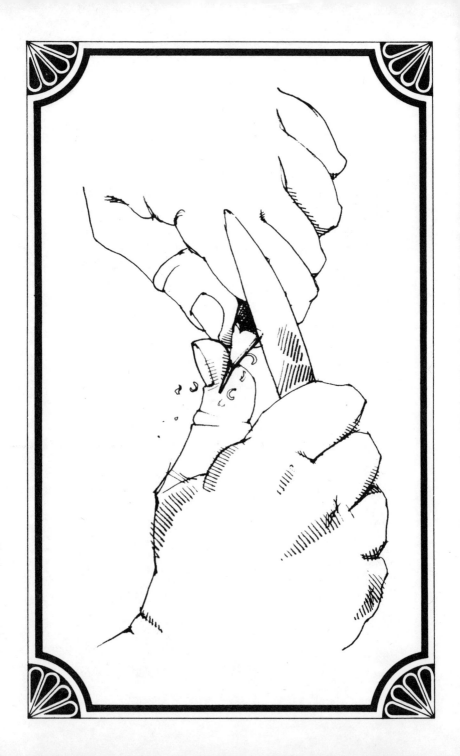

THE PENCIL
SHARPENER

This is a pencil sharpener. The pencil sharpener under discussion is not a machine but a person. (There was a pencil sharpening machine in school, but as far as we knew, it was the only one in the world.)

Grandfathers were particularly good for pencil sharpening, if you happened to have a grandfather around the house. If you didn't have a grandfather handy, you went to the man on the block (usually someone else's grandfather) who had a reputation in the field. They all held the point of the pencil against the thumb, or the ball of the palm, and did what we had all been told not to do—move the knife toward the hand. He shaved minutely, revolving the pencil, until he had produced a minor miracle, cone-shaped, smooth, and so perfect you were loath to use it.

If you couldn't find a grandfather, you had to ask your mother to sharpen a pencil for you, which she did with a kitchen knife, sweeping the end with long, strong strokes and producing, let us be honest, a mess. My father, who couldn't sharpen a pencil worth a damn, was a man of sudden and strange enthusiasms. He was incapable of passing stationery store, hardware store, and fruit store windows. One day he made the grand slam and came home with a typewriter, a pencil sharpener, a spiral screwdriver, and six pomegranates.

He used the screwdriver to mount the pencil sharpener on the back of the kitchen closet door, next to the coffee grinder. And with it, the family entered the industrial revolution and lost some romance.

We thought the pomegranates were terrible.

MEDICINE

This is a prescription. In the first place, there was a giant drug combine known as the kitchen. Here various time-proven remedies were assembled, to be shoved down the weak gullet of the patient. Camomile tea, senna pod tea, mint tea, catnip tea, a compound of honey and glycerin with a nauseous quarter lemon suspended in it.

Here mustard plasters were built, here antiphlogistons melted, here occasionally goose grease was rendered. All these cured heavy chest colds indifferently well, even as today's miracle drugs.

Certain time-tested recipes came from the drugstore, something which was either Doctor Brown's Cough Mixture or Doctors' brown cough mixture, Dobel's solution, a kind of wonderful lead-smelling embrocation for sprains, Citrate of Magnesia, which would purge the hell out of you if it could be gotten past your involuntarily clenched jaws.

Once in a while, a prescription. If liquid, this came in a small bottle, its cork covered by a little cap of pleated paper, tied with a red silk thread. Pills, I think, even then were factory-made, but capsules were compounded by the druggist as were the powders which came in little folded paper packages, some blue, some white. These always fizzed when put together in a glass of water.

There were no tranquilizers then, but lots of ladies went around half-gassed all day on Lydia Pinkham's and lots of old gents were on bitters, a sovereign stomachic which proved out about 80 percent alcohol.

THE
ONYX ASHTRAY

This is an onyx ashtray. Another early sign of afflu-
ence that came from out of nowhere to our town
was the onyx ashtray. I had always thought onyx
was black, but these were called onyx and looked
like an uneasily swirled, nasty green solidified mixture of marshmallow syrup and brake fluid.

Most of them were round or elliptical, and none
of them had cigarette grooves, although many of
them had brass brackets for large cigars. A very
few of them were not turned and polished on the

115

outside, but left in the original rough stone, which made them the first free-form objects.

Many of them were adorned, always in Near-Eastern style. Small bronze camels, small bronze palm trees, and arrangements of camels and palm trees.

The supreme achievement was the seated figure of a man with a turban, displaying a highly colored prayer rug. The rug was molded in a pattern, and the depressions were filled with tiny flecks of different-colored paint.

It was the hobby of every right-minded child —and not a few adults—to pick out the flecks of paint with a pin.

 **LAUNDRY SOAP**

This is a bar of laundry soap. When you bathed, it was usually a big bar of Ivory broken in two, or Fairy soap. (In those innocent times you could have an advertising slogan that read "Do you have a little Fairy in your home?")

I don't recall ever having seen a new bar of laundry soap, it was always an eroded chunk about five inches by three inches, thin at the edges, sand-colored. The name Kirkman's swims uneasily in my mind, but I'm not taking any bets. Laundry soap was reputed to be a sovereign cure for poison

ivy. It was rubbed, dry, all over all the parts of you that had poison ivy. I don't think it cured poison ivy, but as far as I can tell, from reading what the doctors say, nothing cures poison ivy. I wish to make it clear that this cure was not the ignorant belief of small children. It was the accepted, adult, doctor-approved cure.

While I'm at it, I have to tell you about another universally held belief that I have never been able to make any sense out of. The belief was that wearing your rubber indoors would hurt your eyesight. I can't get a hold of any part of that one.

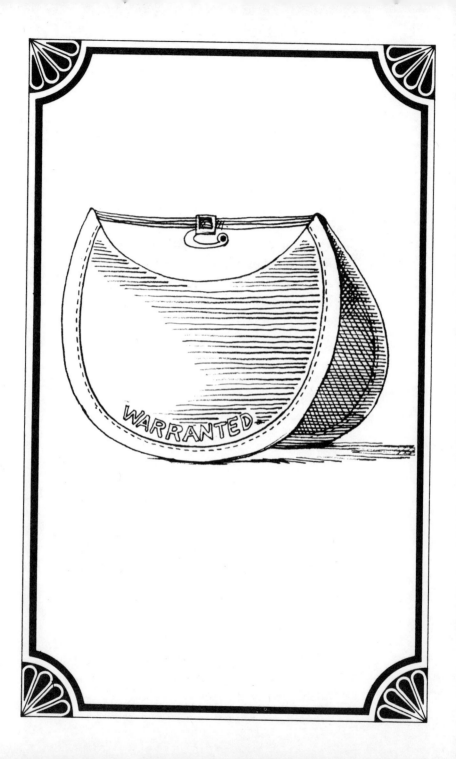

THE
DRESS SHIELD

This is a very delicate subject, for in those days people were much more private about their personal functions. It was still said in those days "Horses sweat, men perspire, ladies glow."

Well, it was a nice ideal, but the fact of the matter was that ladies did indeed sweat. The chief problems, then as now, were the underarms, and the most delicately glowing of ladies, who dabbed genteelly at her upper lip with a handkerchief, was all too aware of two growing spots of damp on her brand-new dotted swiss. The next day she might become aware that it was ruined beyond hope.

Thus the dress shield, a crescent-shaped piece of varnished cloth. It was sewed into the dress, taken out and laundered, and replaced.

And as long as the shield continued to work, ladies continued to glow.

THE
STOP AND GO SIGN

This is a stop and go sign. There wasn't much of an automobile traffic problem in my home town, nor did the trolley cars constitute a difficulty.

What traffic there was, was controlled by a couple of cops on a couple of corners, and down around Fourth Avenue was the only place automation had set in. The policeman there manned a machine made of pipe and sheet metal, a vertical pole bearing two signs, one saying STOP STOP and the other GO GO, at right angles to each other. The pole was pivoted at the bottom and a handle

stuck out at the height of the cop's hand, and on his judgment you stopped or went.

At some point, it was decided to be modern and have traffic lights. The discussion raged for a while—most people believing that no free-born citizen would pay any attention to a traffic signal without a cop.

The other traffic signs I remember were those saying GO SLOW. Each year we were instructed by our teachers that this was poor grammar, and one teacher petitioned annually to have them read GO SLOWLY.

THE LAUNDRY

This is a laundry. The laundry was in the cellar, and it contained a large copper tub, which sat on a two-burner gas stove. It was set to boiling and clothes were dumped in it and boiled, and stirred around with a piece of broom handle. There were two soapstone tubs with faucets, and in one of them clothes were washed with soap, and in the other the soap was rinsed out.

After the boiling, there was another torture for laundry, the washboard, a sheet of corrugated zinc in a wooden frame. This was put in one of the tubs, and what had not, I guess, been boiled out or washed out, was scrubbed out.

The next trial by laundry was the wringer, two large white rubber rollers mounted in a wooden frame equipped with a crank, and clamped onto one of the sinks. Clothes were turned damp from wringing wet in the wringer. (For kids it was a very good thing to send things through and see what they looked like flattened.)

At some point in the process, a bluing cube came into play. It is confused in my mind with the cube of chalk I later used on pool cues, but I think it was bigger and was tied up in a little piece of gauze.

I never asked then why it was used, so many things in my childhood were just plain so, and I learned later that adding blue to white things made them look whiter. I don't begin to understand this.

When the Macbethian witches had ceased boiling the pot, and the laundry had been wrung, it was taken out into the backyard and hung on the clothesline, which in our case was strung around four poles set in a square.

From then on it was at the mercy of rain, dogs, and small children who found ecstasy in running face first into damp, clean-smelling sheets.

That was on Mondays. It is perfectly true that everybody did wash on Monday (maybe they still do) and ironing on Tuesday.

I do believe that a lady who did her wash on Wednesdays and her ironing on Friday would have been brought before a drumhead court martial.

STUFFED BIRDS AND FISH

This is a stuffed owl. A common artifact in the suburban houses of the time were stuffed animals of various genera. I suppose some of them were hunting trophies of the man of the house—as the lunging pickerel was in mine—but certainly my father never used a gun, and the stuffed deer head on the porch, the pheasant, owl, and Baltimore oriole in the living room could only be attributed to his fatal weakness, an inability to look in the window of any store that held things he had never seen before, and not go into those shops. Or perhaps

131

the taxidermist who mounted his fish, complete with hook and spoon, had a display in his studio.

In any event there was the deer head and the birds. The deer head frightened me, it looked so damn alive, and the way it was hung against the wall, I was never sure the body was not on the other side.

I got hollered at for touching the pheasant; I could not resist stroking the long tail feathers, and it got a little tatty at the end.

But the owl was a total delight. Certainly nothing in the world, now or then, was so delicious to touch as the delicate breast feathers. And somehow, the owl did not seem so dead as the other birds. The oriole was just a feather-covered sack, and the pheasant, like live pheasants, seemed more a jeweled toy than a real living thing.

The pickerel was mounted on a wood plaque, in an anguished arc, with the hook and spoon on a taut line to his jaw, and it hurt to look at it.

The most obscene of all stuffed beasts was an arrangement in someone else's house. Some very sick taxidermist had stuffed frogs and arranged them around a poker table, with miniature cards and glasses, and had put tiny cigars in their mouths. It is a skill that I pray has been lost.

SMOKES

This is a smoke. Men smoked cigars or pipes, Italian men smoked Italian stogies (Italian stogies looked as if they'd been dipped in ink and they burned as if they'd been dipped in gun powder). Dudes smoked cigarettes. It was considered not manly. It was not considered womanly either, and as a general rule the few women who smoked smoked only in their own homes. A woman who lit a cigarette in a restaurant was like as not asked to leave.

Kids smoked anything. Stolen cigars, stolen

cigarettes, cigarettes made of corn silk rolled up in newspaper, dried tea leaves ditto. There was a plant that grew in the vacant corner lots, and its stem was woody and porous, and we cut that up and smoked that. (For all I know, it may have been marijuana, and if we had dried the leaves before we smoked them, we might never have gotten hooked on cigarettes.)

Although a lot of people smoked cigarettes then, they didn't smoke a lot of cigarettes. They often were carried in cases, which held ten or so, and in the cigar stores there was an open, lidless cigar box full of loose cigarettes, which sold for, I think, a penny each.

Cigarettes were considered even then to be dangerous, the common bravado term among cigarette smokers being coffin nails.

You were told that smoking cigarettes would stunt your growth (parents told you anything that they didn't want you to do would stunt your growth) and you were promised rewards varying from a dollar watch to an Orient Buckboard if you would not smoke until you were twenty-one.

It did about as much good then as what we're doing does now.

THE STAINED GLASS WINDOW

This is a stained-glass window. There was a landing on the stairs, and on the landing was a stained-glass window.

If you were young enough, and simple enough, you could spend up to half an hour stretching, bending, and swaying and dyeing the world green, blue, ruby red, amber.

Lots of houses had stained-glass windows in the bathrooms, for privacy, but the one on the landing seemed to have been put there for the sheer joy of it. Sometimes the sun shone in, and the floor was covered with pools of color, like a transparent rug.

It was as pleasant a window as I have ever seen in my life.

THE SOAP
SCRAP SAVER

This is a soap scrap saver. It is a little wire cage with two handles on it. You opened it up and put in it whatever little bits of soap were too small for your hands to keep hold of.

You have to remember that in those days you bathed with soap, did dishes with soap, did laundry with soap, and it all came in bars. (Except for green soap, which came in bottles and was primarily for shampooing, secondarily for getting in your eyes.) There were no soap flakes, and there were no synthetic detergents.

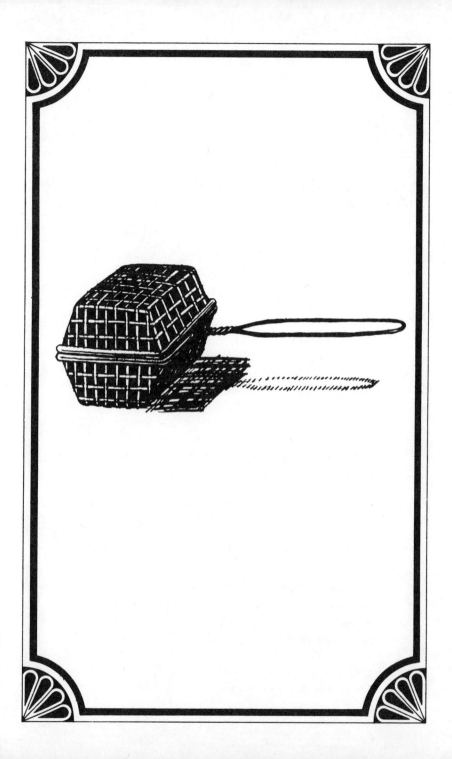

All the little superannuated pieces of soap were put in the soap scrap saver, and it was whipped around in the kitchen sink to do the dishes.

After you washed the dishes you had to dry them. Like all right-minded people, we wiped the dishes dry. My uncle, who taught chemistry, told my mother that laboratory glasses were rinsed in hot water and left to dry on racks. He suggested she do that with the dishes. She paid absolutely no attention to this cockeyed notion. She said it was dirty and we went on wiping them with moderately clean dish towels.

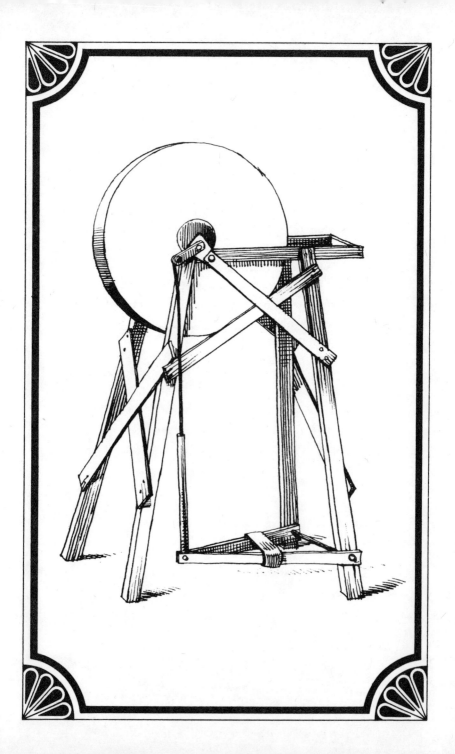

THE
KNIFE GRINDER

This is a knife grinder. I can hardly believe I used
to see this. It seems like something out of a Breughel
drawing, but I know I did see it.

First you heard the hand-rung brass bell tolling
and then you saw a man walking, bent nearly double by the weight of a heavy wooden A-frame
with a grind stone on top. He would stop in front
of your house, straighten up slowly, easing the
leather loops off his shoulders, setting the contrap-
tion down on the pavement.

He would go to the back door and be given a

handful of kitchen knives and maybe a scissors.

There was a foot treadle that turned the crank, and a little metal cone on top of the wheel filled with water and plugged at the point with a piece of rag, so that the water trickled down sparingly.

Wonderful sparks came off the wheel, long thin lines of light that burst at the end into hair thin petals.

I know I saw all this, but what is hard to believe is that in my lifetime, in my home town, in my country, a man walked day after day all over town bearing such a burden on his back.

Many years later on, in the suburb in which I raised my children, a sort of small converted bus used to make the same rounds. The rear of the bus was a small shop with an assortment of grinding wheels run, I think, by electricity generated by the bus motor.

The bus was way above a child's point of view, so no kid ever saw those sparks.

But more than equally, no kid ever saw a man bent double, probably permanently.

It would be nice to think that the man with the bus was the son of the man with the wheel on his back. I think I will think so.

THE GAS LAMP

This is a gas lamp. The lamplighter is another thing like the knife-grinder, so antique it doesn't seem possible that I saw it. But I did.

I did not live in the gaslight era, at least not in the house. Many years later, as an adult, I lived in an old house that had retained its gaslight after the installation of electricity, a thing you could not trust.

But as I say, in my house and the houses of all my peers, electricity was an accepted thing.

Then why were the street lights gas, and why,

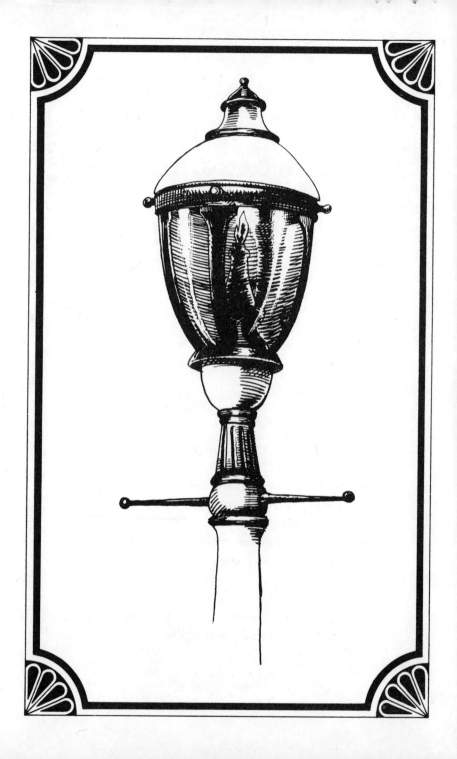

every dusk, did a man come along the block carrying a mysterious pole that he poked into the egg-cup-shaped glass bowl of the street light, producing first a blue flame and then a yellow glow?

The pole seemed to have a metal fitting at the top, two-branched. I know that one end of this turned on the gas, but the other end remains a mystery to me to this day. I can only presume it had some sort of sparking wheel on it, because I do not remember that as he carried the pole there was any light on it.

I think part of the reason I am so stupid about this is that it existed only when I was very small (there must have been conversion to electricity at some point) and when you are very small you accept all kinds of magic as perfectly normal.

The other thing that complicates this memory is that at about the same time I had read to me a Robert Louis Stevenson poem called "Leary The Lamplighter." I knew then and know now that I am not as old as Robert Louis Stevenson, and each time I remember the lamps going on a horrible doubt seizes me: am I remembering my block or am I remembering the poem?

No, no, I am sure. I can see him.

Now it occurs to me that he must have turned them off, too, but I never saw that. Perhaps if he turned them on at dusk he turned them off at dawn when only the milkman was on the street.

GLUE AND OTHER STICKY MATTER

This is about glue and paste and tape. There were certain sticky things around a household, primarily surgical in nature, that took on other uses. For a very small cut in our house we used court plaster, thin black silk with a gummy back that you licked and stuck on. The other use of court plaster (from which I guess it took its name) was that ladies cut out tiny circles or crescents. With full evening dress, one of these was stuck on the face, usually on the cheek. The theory was that the black of the beauty spots enhanced the whiteness of the skin.

149

For cuts requiring more than court plaster, adhesive tape was used. (Another one of the miraculous things mothers did was to tear the adhesive straight across.) Adhesive tape had two other functions. It was the drug of choice for padding the bridge of the brass wire spectacles which were common then and also to repair spectacles when the earpieces came undone at the hinge. It was also used, if you could get away with it, for wrapping the handle of a tennis racket. The handles of baseball bats were bound with friction tape, which lived in the garage. There was a baseball called a nickel rocket, that cost a dime. It would survive about six glancing blows, at which point it came apart at the seams. The game was called, and the ball was wound elaborately with at least two layers of friction tape, lasted forever, and weighed about twice as much.

Paste, which you made yourself from flour and water and a little salt, was used on one's private projects, like making a kite. In school, and sometimes in homes, there was a jar of library paste. The jar was a big squat glass cylinder, and the screw top had a little hollow pillar on top. There was a similar hollow well inside that held the brush. The well was entirely surrounded by white paste. You filled the well with water, dipped the brush in and ran it around the paste, and went about your business.

Then there was mucilage, which was a way station between paste and glue, and had what we thought was a very funny name.

And now, at long last, glue.

There were usually a number of bottles of glue at the back of the workbench in the cellar. We knew they were very good glues. They came in little flat bottles and usually had a screw top with a built in brush. We knew they were very good, because most times we found the metal cap permanently welded to the bottle. (Once in a while we got one open, and found the brush firmly bound in the age-thickened glue. But somehow or other, we managed.) There was a glue called MacCormack's Iron Glue, but never having any reason to glue iron, we left it alone.

But the real first-water, triple-distilled—the real McCoy of glues was hot glue.

This was used for really important jobs, like gluing a Morris chair back together, or the splats (sic) of a Windsor chair, or assembling something important that you had built. There were two kinds—fish glue and rabbit skin, and some swore by one, some by the other. In one respect, there was little to choose. Both raised a stink unequalled in the world of aroma. Fish glue came in slabs the color and general contour of burned peanut brittle without the peanuts. You broke off bits, which at this stage of the game were only slightly gamey, and put them in a battered old saucepan consecrated to glue.

In most cellars there was a one or two burner gas stove: its primary use was boiling starch.

Well, with heat the glue not only liquefied, but sent forth an atmosphere that filled the place solid.

You put the hot glue where it was needed, and you broke for the open—fragrant to the nth degree.

Dogs threw back their heads and bayed when you passed and people looked at you suspiciously. Your mouth tasted like glue and your meals were glue for a day and a half.

The claim of people who used hot glue was that the joint was stronger than the wood itself. This was perfectly true.

THE
WASHBOARD BAND

This is a washboard. Some of us took music
lessons: on the piano or the violin, when we would
have sold our souls for a trumpet or trombone.

We would have been drawn and quartered
before we'd play "The Happy Farmer" or "Country
Gardens" in public, but of our own free will we
operated a washboard band in full view and earshot
of our contemporaries. First, we had to steal the
components: a washboard, a number of thimbles,
a galvanized iron washtub, a broomstick, the kind
of cord that carpenters rubbed against chalk and

153

used as a marking snap-line, some jugs, and two dry marrow bones.

The washtub was upended, and a hole drilled in it. The chalk line was put through it and knotted on the inside, the other end was tied to the top of the broomstick. The bottom of the broomstick was wedged against the ridge of the washtub, and by tightening and loosening the cord, and plucking, a sort of string bass was produced.

The jugs were of various sizes, and by blowing across the top of them, further sound was added. The thimbles were put on the fingers of both hands, and by rubbing them up and down the washboard, something resembling a real drummer's rim shots was attained.

The marrow bones were allowed to dry, cut to the same length and held between the fingers of one hand. They made a clacking sound, and a skillful marrow bone player could produce considerable syncopation. (You see this once in a while on television, done with spoons.)

So there was a hell of a lot of rhythm going. But, you ask, where was the melody?

You may well ask.

THE RUMBLE SEAT

This is a rumble seat. Model A Fords, and many other cars that few of us had the opportunity to ride in, had a hinged cover on the back deck, which, when opened, disclosed a tight-fitting seat for two slim people.

It was sometimes called the mother-in-law seat (by the way, I have no idea why it was called the rumble seat, that was just what it was named), but to me and my friends, it had nothing to do with mothers-in-law.

It had to do with sex. The size of the rumble

seat enforced a certain intimacy, and any girl who got in one had a pretty clear idea that she would be kissed, hugged, and have anything grabbable grabbed.

You heard that the final intimacy had been attained in a rumble seat, usuallv from one of the many habitual liars among your companions.

I categorically state (and await a flood of protest from those same grown-up liars) that this was a mechanical impossibility.

The fact of the matter is that with a steering wheel, gear shifts, and emergency brakes, it was no cinch in the front seat, and often the pain outdid the pleasure.

ABOUT
THE AUTHOR

Robert Paul Smith is an aging writer.

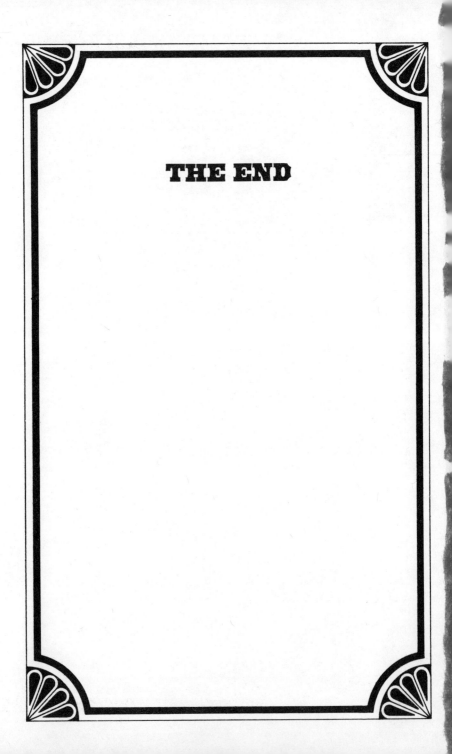

THE END